Spider Names

Susan Canizares

Scholastic Inc.

New York • Toronto • London • Auckland • Sydney

Acknowledgments

Science Consultants: Patrick R. Thomas, Ph.D., Bronx Zoo/Wildlife Conservation Park; Glenn Phillips, The New York Botanical Garden; **Literacy Specialist:** Maria Utefsky, Reading Recovery Coordinator, District 2, New York City

Design: MKR Design, Inc.

Photo Research: Barbara Scott

Endnotes: Susan Russell

Photographs: Cover: John R. MacGregor/Peter Arnold, Inc.; p. 1: (bl): Robert & Linda Mitchell, (tl): Gilbert S. Grant/Photo Researchers, Inc., (tr): Hans Pfletschinger/ Peter Arnold, Inc., (br): S. Camazine & K. Visscher/Photo Researchers, Inc.; p. 2: S. J. Krasemann/Peter Arnold, Inc.; p. 3: Hans Pfletschinger/Peter Arnold, Inc.; p. 4 & 5: Robert & Linda Mitchell; p. 6: Zefa/ The Stock Market; p. 7: John R. MacGregor; p. 8: Don Mason/The Stock Market; p. 9: S. Camazine & K. Visscher/ Photo Researchers, Inc.; p. 10: Cesar Paredes/ The Stock Market; p. 11: Michael Fogden/DRK Photo; p. 12: Gilbert S. Grant/Photo Researchers, Inc.

Library of Congress Cataloging-in-Publication Data
Canizares, Susan, 1960-
Spider names / Susan Canizares.
p. cm. -- (Science emergent readers)
"Scholastic early childhood."
Includes index.
Summary: Photographs and simple text explain how different species of spiders got their names.
ISBN 0-590-39795-8 (pbk.: alk. paper)
1. Spider--Nomenclature (Popular)--Juvenile literature. [1. Spiders.]
I. Canizares, Susan, 1960-. II. Title. III. Series.
QL458.4.C345 1998

595.4'4--dc21

97-29197
CIP AC

20   19   18   17   16   15   14   03   02   01

What are their names?

crab

crab spider

ant

ant spider

wolf

wolf spider

violin

violin spider

wheel

wheel spider

You give it a **name!**

Spider Names

There are more than 30,000 species of spiders in the world. They are not insects because, among other reasons, they have eight legs instead of six and no wings. They are all carnivorous, eating prey they have hunted or trapped. Their food is usually insects, often ones that are destructive to human habitats and food. This makes them good friends to people. Many of them trap their food in the amazing webs they weave, but some are excellent hunters. We've named spiders in ways that help us recognize them. Which is your favorite?

The Crab Spider gets its name because it looks like a tiny crab and because it moves like a crab, with a sideways, scuttling motion. The Crab Spider doesn't spin webs; instead, it crouches, waits, and pounces on its prey, killing it with a poisonous bite.

The whole name of the Ant Spider is the Ant Mimic Spider. It gets its name because it looks and acts just like an ant. It is so good at pretending to be an ant that it is able to hide among them in their nests. This way it can easily attack and eat them.

The Wolf Spider uses its keen eyesight to hunt for food during the day. It has six eyes in the front and two at the top that help it see toward the sides and back. It gets its name because it attacks like a wolf, creeping up warily and then putting on a burst of speed and leaping onto its prey.

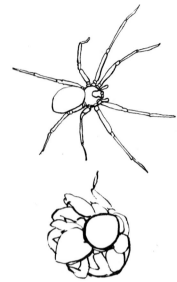

The Violin Spider gets its name from the violin-shaped mark on its body. It comes from the family of "recluse" spiders, and it can be dangerous to people. It is usually brown and small and hard to see. It is very shy, doesn't like the light, and hides under woodpiles or rocks. If it has to bite in self-defense, its poison can make a person very sick.

The Wheel Spider lives in the desert and gets its name from the way it moves. When it wants to escape from an enemy, it gathers in its legs and becomes round. Then the desert wind rolls it quickly away, like a tiny wheel.

The Marbled Orb Weaver is named for the way in which it spins its web. After making the silk structure, the spider walks in a circle, creating the spirals that finish the web shape. The web is almost invisible and sticky, too! It catches any insects that fly into it by mistake and holds them for the spider to kill and eat.